JOHN F. KENNEDY

IN "QUOTES"

INSPIRATION AND RHETORIC FROM THE USA'S ICONIC LEADER

JOHN F. KENNEDY

IN "QUOTES"

INSPIRATION AND RHETORIC FROM THE USA'S ICONIC LEADER

PRESS
ASSOCIATION
Images

First published 2013 by
Ammonite Press
an imprint of AE Publications Ltd,
166 High Street, Lewes, East Sussex, BN7 1XU, United Kingdom

Images © Press Association, 2013
Copyright © in the Work AE Publications Ltd, 2013

ISBN 978-1-78145-058-1

This publication contains extracts of texts and images which have been compiled from a variety of sources for the purpose of providing
criticism and review of the subject matter to which this publication relates.

While we have made strenuous efforts to include appropriate acknowledgements in this book,
the publishers will be pleased to hear from anyone who has not been appropriately acknowledged, and to make a correction in future reprints.

British Cataloguing in Publication Data. A catalogue record of this book is available
from the British Library.

Series Editor: Richard Wiles
Designer: Robin Shields
Picture research: Press Association/Associated Press

Colour reproduction by GMC Reprographics
Printed in China

"Let us never negotiate out of fear. But let us never fear to negotiate."

Inaugural Address, Washington, DC, 20th January, 1961

President John F. Kennedy and his wife Jacqueline leave the airport at West Palm Beach, Florida, for the home of friends where they will spend a short break. 11th May, 1961

"A man may die, nations may rise and fall, but an idea lives on. Ideas have endurance without death."

Recorded for the commissioning of a United States Information Agency transmitter at Greenville, North Carolina, 8th February, 1963

This bronze statue of President John F. Kennedy stands in Fort Worth, Texas, near the spot where he gave one of his last two public speeches on the day he was killed. 8th November, 2012

Introduction

At 12.30pm on Friday 22nd November, 1963, shots rang out in a downtown plaza in Dallas, Texas. A man riding with his pretty young wife in the back of an open limousine slumped forward, fatally wounded. Onlookers were horrified, but the shock waves of the man's death would reverberate around the world. He was John F. Kennedy, and he was the President of the United States.

Kennedy came from a 'political' family with Irish roots. Before entering politics, however, young 'Jack' had served with the US Navy during the Second World War. He had commanded a torpedo boat in the Pacific and had been highly decorated for bravery following the sinking of his boat. Discharged from the Navy with a chronic back injury that would plague him for the rest of his life, he became a Democratic Congressman and eventually entered the Senate in 1953. That year, he also married the beautiful Jacqueline Bouvier. Kennedy received the Democratic Party's nomination for president in 1960 and narrowly beat Republican Richard Nixon, assuming the office at the beginning of 1961. At 46, he became the youngest ever elected president.

In a world used to 'stuffy' aged senior politicians, the charismatic Kennedys brought glamour to the White House and garnered worldwide popularity. But there was more to Kennedy's administration than glitz: he instituted economic programmes that led to the longest period of sustained growth in the United States since the war; he worked vigorously for civil rights; and he took action to counter the challenge of Communism in Europe, Southeast Asia and Cuba.

To this day, controversy surrounds the assassination of John F. Kennedy. Officially, he was shot by a lone gunman, Lee Harvey Oswald, but many believe there was a conspiracy. Because his life was cut short so tragically, we can never know whether he would have won a second term in office, whether he would have gone down in history as a great president or become a revered elder statesman. Like all men, he was flawed, being given to philandering, but his popularity among US presidents remains very high.

Illustrated with contemporary news photographs from the archives of the Press Association and Associated Press, this book is a celebration of John F. Kennedy in his own words.

US Ambassador to Great Britain Joseph P. Kennedy (C) and his sons Joseph P. Kennedy, Jr (L) and John F. Kennedy aboard an ocean liner.

1938

"I just received the following wire from my generous Daddy: 'Dear Jack, Don't buy a single vote more than is necessary. I'll be damned if I'm going to pay for a landslide.'"

Remarks at Gridiron Dinner, Washington, DC, 15th March, 1958

"It was involuntary. They sank my boat."

When asked how he became a hero in the Second World War. Quoted by Arthur M. Schlesinger in *A Thousand Days: John F. Kennedy in the White House*, 1965

A young Lieutenant John F. Kennedy during his time as skipper of a US Navy torpedo boat in the Pacific during the Second World War. 1943

"War will exist until that distant day when the conscientious objector enjoys the same reputation and prestige that the warrior does today."

Undated letter to a naval friend, quoted by Arthur M. Schlesinger in *A Thousand Days: John F. Kennedy in the White House*, 1965

Lieutenant John F. Kennedy takes a break from his naval duties at the Stork Club in New York City. 9th February, 1944

"I hope that no American will waste his franchise and throw away his vote by voting either for me or against me solely on account of my religious affiliation. It is not relevant."

President John. F. Kennedy and his wife Jacqueline leave St Francis Xavier Church in Hyannis, Massachusetts, after attending mass. The couple had a summer home at nearby Hyannis Port.
27th August, 1961

"A man does what he must – in spite of personal consequences, in spite of obstacles and dangers, and pressures – and that is the basis of all human morality."

Profiles in Courage, 1956

Senator John F. Kennedy with his wife Jacqueline on the steps of the Senate in Washington, DC. He was returning to work after a long absence for treatment of a wartime spinal injury.
23rd May, 1955

"The stories of past courage … can teach, they can offer hope, they can provide inspiration. But they cannot provide courage itself. For this each man must look into his own soul."

Profiles in Courage, 1956

Senator John F. Kennedy in his office in Washington, DC.
26th July, 1956

"Let us not seek the Republican answer or the Democratic answer, but the right answer. Let us not seek to fix the blame for the past. Let us accept our own responsibility for the future."

Speech, Loyola College Alumni Banquet, Baltimore, Maryland, 18th February, 1958

Senator John F. Kennedy of Massachusetts and his wife Jacqueline celebrate in Boston following the news that he had won re-election by a record margin. 5th November, 1958

"The Chinese use two brush strokes to write the word 'crisis'. One brush stroke stands for danger; the other for opportunity. In a crisis, be aware of the danger – but recognise the opportunity."

Speech, Indianapolis, Indiana, 12th April, 1959

Senator John F. Kennedy (R) confers with his brothers, Edward (C) and Robert, Counsel for the Senate Rackets Committee, during a committee hearing in Washington, DC.
1959

"We can have faith in the future only if we have faith in ourselves."

Presidential nomination acceptance speech, 15th July, 1960

At home in Washington, DC, the Democratic Senator for Massachusetts, John F. Kennedy, reads newspaper reports of his Presidential Primary election victory over Hubert Humphrey in West Virginia. 11th May, 1960

The News

JACK KENNEDY'S ON
THE GLORY ROAD
Humphrey Bows Out

Russia Implies Threat

"I appreciate your welcome. As the cow said to the Maine farmer, 'Thank you for a warm hand on a cold morning.'"

Response to an enthusiastic crowd in Los Angeles, California.

Senator John F. Kennedy makes his way through a crowd of supporters and journalists after arriving in Los Angeles, California, for the Democratic national convention.
9th July, 1960

"We stand today on the edge of a new frontier – the frontier of the 1960s – a frontier of unknown opportunities and perils – a frontier of unfulfilled hopes and threats."

Presidential nomination acceptance speech, 15th July, 1960

Senator John F. Kennedy makes a speech during his presidential campaign.
1960

"The only valid test of leadership is the ability to lead, and lead vigorously."

Presidential nomination acceptance speech, 15th July, 1960

John F. Kennedy makes a brief speech during the Democratic Party's national convention in Los Angeles, California, where he would be nominated as the party's presidential candidate. At left is his sister Patricia, who was married to actor Peter Lawford. 14th July, 1960

DEMOCRATIC NATIONAL CONVENTION 1960

"**All of us have in our veins the exact same percentage of salt in our blood that exists in the ocean, and, therefore, we have salt in our blood, in our sweat, in our tears. We are tied to the ocean. And when we go back to the sea – whether it is to sail or to watch it – we are going back from whence we came.**"

Remarks at Australian Ambassador's dinner for America's Cup crews, Newport, Rhode Island, 14th September, 1962

Senator John F. Kennedy and his wife Jacqueline set out to sail around Nantucket Sound at Hyannis Port aboard the family yacht *Marlin*.
19th July, 1960

"We celebrate the past to awaken the future."

Remarks at the 25th anniversary of the signing of the Social Security Act,
Hyde Park, New York, 14th August, 1960

Senator John F. Kennedy waves to the crowd before making a speech in
front of the Alamo, the shrine to Texan liberty, in San Antonio, Texas.
12th September, 1960

"Do you realise the responsibility I carry? I'm the only person standing between Richard Nixon and the White House."

Quoted by Arthur M. Schlesinger in *A Thousand Days: John F. Kennedy in the White House*, 1965

Presidential candidates Senator John F. Kennedy (L) and Vice President Richard M. Nixon (R) are greeted by Francis Cardinal Spellman at the Alfred E. Smith Memorial Dinner at New York's Waldorf Astoria. 19th October, 1960

"I believe there can only be one defence policy for the United States and that is summed up in the word 'first'. I do not mean first, *but*. I do not mean first, *when*. I do not mean first, *if*. I mean first – period!"

Speech, Veterans of Foreign Wars Convention, Detroit, Michigan, 26th August, 1960

President-elect John F. Kennedy (R) is greeted by his running mate, Vice President-elect Lyndon B. Johnson, upon arrival at the latter's ranch near Johnson City, Texas.
16th November, 1960

"Leadership and learning are indispensable to each other."

President-elect John F. Kennedy (R) discusses the hand-over of power with President Dwight D. Eisenhower at the White House in Washington, DC.
6th December, 1960

"Let the word go forth from this time and place, to friend and foe alike, that the torch has been passed to a new generation of Americans."

Inaugural Address, Washington, DC, 20th January, 1961

President-elect John F. Kennedy works on the draft of his inaugural speech as he flies from New York to Washington, DC, for the inauguration ceremony. 18th January, 1961

"If we are strong, our strength will speak for itself. If we are weak, words will be of no help."

Chief Justice Earl Warren (centre, L) administers the oath of office to President John F. Kennedy (centre, R) in Washington, DC. Vice President Lyndon B. Johnson can be seen immediately behind Kennedy, with Richard M. Nixon at far right. 20th January, 1961

"Let every nation know, whether it wishes us well or ill, that we shall pay any price, bear any burden, meet any hardship, support any friend, oppose any foe to assure the survival and the success of liberty."

Inaugural Address, Washington, DC, 20th January, 1961

President John F. Kennedy delivers his inaugural address after taking
the oath of office at the Capitol building in Washington, DC.
20th January, 1961

"Now the trumpet summons us again – not as a call to bear arms, though arms we need; not as a call to battle, though embattled we are – but a call to bear the burden of a long twilight struggle, year in and year out, 'rejoicing in hope, patient in tribulation' – a struggle against the common enemies of man: tyranny, poverty, disease and war itself."

Inaugural Address, Washington, DC, 20th January, 1961

President John F. Kennedy and his wife Jacqueline are driven along Constitution Avenue in Washington, DC, during the new president's inauguration parade.
20th January, 1961

"The world is very different now. For man holds in his mortal hands the power to abolish all forms of human poverty, and all forms of human life."

Inaugural Address, Washington, DC, 20th January, 1961

President John F. Kennedy on his first day in office.
21st January, 1961

"And so, my fellow Americans: ask not what your country can do for you – ask what you can do for your country. My fellow citizens of the world: ask not what America will do for you, but what together we can do for the freedom of man."

Inaugural Address, Washington, DC, 20th January, 1961

President John F. Kennedy and members of his cabinet at the White House in Washington, DC. L–R: Edward Day (Postmaster General), Adlai Stevenson (UN Ambassador), Lyndon B. Johnson (Vice President), Robert McNamara (Defence), Orville Freeman (Agriculture), Arthur Goldberg (Labour), Abraham Ribicoff (Welfare), Luther Hodges (Commerce), Robert Kennedy (Attorney General), Dean Rusk (State), President Kennedy, Douglas Dillon (Treasury), Stewart Udall (Interior). 26th January, 1961

"If a free society cannot help the many who are poor, it cannot save the few who are rich."

Inaugural Address, Washington, DC, 20th January, 1961

President John F. Kennedy makes the throw to open the major-league
baseball season at Griffith Stadium, Washington, DC.
10th April, 1961

"If the self-discipline of the free cannot match the iron discipline of the mailed fist … then the peril to freedom will continue to rise."

Address to the American Society of Newspaper Editors, Washington, DC, 20th April, 1961

President John F. Kennedy and Vice President Lyndon B. Johnson (L) watch the action during the American League baseball season opener between the Chicago White Sox and Washington Senators. 10th April, 1961

JOHN F. KENNEDY IN QUOTES **57**

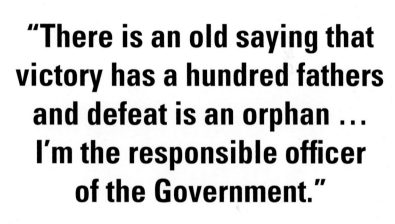

"There is an old saying that victory has a hundred fathers and defeat is an orphan ... I'm the responsible officer of the Government."

Press conference following the failed Bay of Pigs invasion of Cuba, sponsored by the United States, 21st April, 1961

President John F. Kennedy studies paperwork with his Appointment Secretary, Kenneth O'Donnell.
22nd April, 1961

"Without debate, without criticism, no Administration and no country can succeed – and no republic can survive."

Address to the American Newspaper Publishers Association, New York, 27th April, 1961

Dignitaries gather for the 15th General Assembly of the United Nations in New York City. L–R: Frederick Boland, President of the Assembly; President John F. Kennedy; Adlai Stevenson, US Ambassador to the UN; Dag Hammarskjöld, Secretary General of the UN. 28th April, 1961

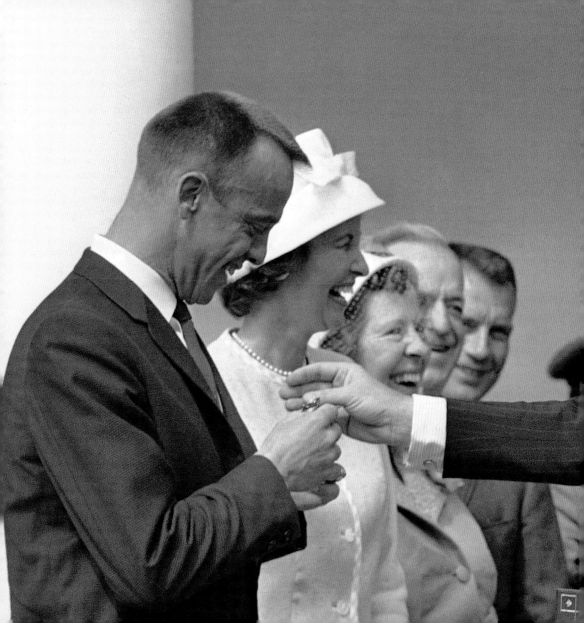

"Only those who dare to fail greatly can ever achieve greatly."

Astronaut Alan B. Shepard is presented with the NASA Distinguished Service Medal by President John F. Kennedy at the White House in Washington, DC. 8th May, 1961

"When we got into office, the thing that surprised me the most was that things were as bad as we'd been saying they were."

President John F. Kennedy and Lady Bird Johnson, wife of Vice President Lyndon B. Johnson (behind Kennedy's left shoulder), share a joke at the microphone during a reception in the White House Rose Garden to welcome the return of the Johnsons following their fact-finding world tour.
24th May, 1961

"No president should fear public scrutiny of his programme. For from that scrutiny comes understanding; and from that understanding comes support or opposition. And both are necessary."

Address to the American Newspaper Publishers Association, New York, 27th April, 1961

President John F. Kennedy meets with Israeli Premier David Ben-Gurion at the Waldorf Hotel in New York City. 30th May, 1961

"I am the man who accompanied Jacqueline Kennedy to Paris, and I have enjoyed it."

Speech, Supreme Headquarters Allied Powers Europe, Paris, France, 2nd June, 1961

First Lady Jacqueline Kennedy and President John F. Kennedy leave the Quai d'Orsay for a reception at the Elysée Palace during their official visit to Paris, France.
31st May, 1961

"The great revolution in the history of man, past, present and future, is the revolution of those determined to be free."

Message to Chairman Khrushchev Concerning the Meaning of Events in Cuba (the Cuban Missile Crisis), 18th April, 1961

Soviet Premier Nikita Khrushchev (L) and President John F. Kennedy during a historic first summit meeting between the two leaders in Vienna, Austria. 3rd June, 1961

"I wonder how it is with you, Harold? If I don't have a woman for three days, I get terrible headaches."

Conversation with British Prime Minister Harold Macmillan, Bermuda, 1961

British Prime Minister Harold Macmillan points out landmarks to President
John F. Kennedy at his Sussex home following informal talks.
30th June, 1963

"A nation that is afraid to let its people judge the truth and falsehood in an open market is a nation that is afraid of its people."

President John F. Kennedy chats with Fulbert Youlou, leader of the Republic of Congo, who had just arrived at Washington airport for a three-day informal visit. 8th June, 1961

"We must never forget that art is not a form of propaganda; it is a form of truth."

Speech upon receiving an honorary degree, Amherst College, Amherst, Massachusetts, 26th October, 1963

William Tolbert (second L), Vice President of Liberia, and Liberian Ambassador George Padmore (second R) present President John F. Kennedy with a tapestry featuring the flags of their two countries. 26th June, 1961

"Chairman Khrushchev … reminds me of the tiger hunter who picked a place on the wall to hang the tiger's skin long before he has caught the tiger. This tiger has other ideas."

News conference, Washington, DC, June, 1961

President John F. Kennedy explains a point during a news conference.
28th June, 1961

"In the long history of the world, only a few generations have been granted the role of defending freedom in its hour of maximum danger. I do not shrink from this responsibility – I welcome it."

Inaugural Address, Washington, DC, 20th January, 1961

President John F. Kennedy (R) walks with Secretary of Defence Robert McNamara toward a pier to board the Kennedy family cruiser at Hyannis Port, Massachusetts. 8th July, 1961

"Do not pray for easy lives. Pray to be stronger men."

President John F. Kennedy ponders a point during a discussion about Berlin with advisors aboard the yacht *Marlin*. L–R: President Kennedy, General Maxwell Taylor, Secretary of State Dean Rusk and Secretary of Defence Robert McNamara.
8th July, 1961

"**Democracy and defence are not substitutes for one another. Either alone will fail.**"

President John F. Kennedy during a news conference at the State Department in Washington, DC.
10th August, 1961

"Mankind must put an end to war or war will put an end to mankind."

Speech, UN General Assembly, New York, 25th September, 1961

President John F. Kennedy addresses the United Nations General Assembly in New York.
25th September, 1961

"We must face the fact that the United States is neither omnipotent nor omniscient – that we are only six per cent of the world's population – that we cannot impose our will upon the other ninety-four per cent of mankind."

Speech, University of Washington, Seattle, Washington, 16th November, 1961

President John F. Kennedy singles out a reporter during a question-and-answer session in Washington, DC. 29th November, 1961

"We must use time as a tool, not as a couch."

Address to National Association of Manufacturers, New York, 5th December, 1961

President John F. Kennedy at his desk in the White House, Washington, DC.
18th January, 1962

"The time to repair the roof is when the sun is shining."

Message to Congress on the State of the Union, 11th January, 1962

President John F. Kennedy in conversation with King Saud of Saudi Arabia at the King's mansion in Palm Beach, Florida.
27th January, 1962

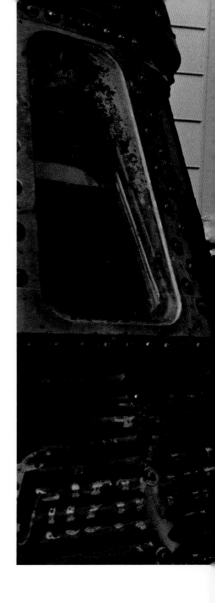

"For one true measure of a nation is its success in fulfilling the promise of a better life for each of its members. Let this be the measure of our nation."

Message to Congress on National Health Needs, 27th February, 1962

Astronaut John Glenn (L) explains the *Friendship 7* spacecraft to President John F. Kennedy and Vice President Lyndon B. Johnson (second R) at the Cape Canaveral space centre in Florida. 23rd February, 1962

"I would rather be accused of breaking precedents than breaking promises."

Florida Senator George Smathers (L) and President John F. Kennedy take their places at a Democratic Party fund raising dinner at Miami Beach, Florida. 10th March, 1962

"Conformity is the jailer of freedom and the enemy of growth."

President John F. Kennedy receives 1962 Easter Seals from Easter Seal Child 10-year-old Tommy Doyle of Manhattan Beach, California. Between them is Mrs Morton B. Phillips, chairwoman of the Easter Seal drive sponsored by the National Society for Crippled Children and Adults. Tommy had brought a ball for the president to autograph. 15th March, 1962

"This nation was founded by men of many nations and backgrounds. It was founded on the principle that all men are created equal, and that the rights of every man are diminished when the rights of one man are threatened."

Radio and TV address on civil rights, 11th June, 1963

President John F. Kennedy and members of Congress enjoy a moment of hilarity during a bill signing ceremony at the White House in Washington, DC. 15th March, 1962

"There is always inequity in life. Some men are killed in a war and some men are wounded, and some men never leave the country. … It's very hard in the military or personal life to assure complete equality. Life is unfair."

News conference, 21st March, 1962

President John F. Kennedy answers questions during a news conference in Washington, DC.
21st March, 1962

"I am reminded of the story of the great French marshal Lyautey, who once asked his gardener to plant a tree. The gardener objected that the tree was slow growing and would not reach maturity for 100 years. The marshal replied, 'In that case, there is not time to lose; plant it this afternoon!'"

Address at the University of California, Berkeley, California, 23rd March, 1962

President John F. Kennedy (C) waves to the crowd at the Memorial Stadium of the University of California, Berkeley, California. The President was the main speaker at the university's Charter Day ceremonies. 23rd March, 1962

"Our problems are man-made, therefore they may be solved by man. No problem of human destiny is beyond human beings."

Major C.W. Simonson (L), commander of a US Air Force missile combat crew, presents President John F. Kennedy with a missile man badge during the president's tour of Vandenberg Air Base, California.
23rd March, 1962

"We set sail on this new sea because there is new knowledge to be gained, and new rights to be won, and they must be won and used for the progress of all people."

Address on the US space effort at Rice University, Houston, Texas, 12th September, 1962

President John F. Kennedy points skyward as he watches an Atlas ballistic missile climb into the sky during a visit to Vandenberg Air Force Base, California. With him are Defence Secretary Robert S. McNamara (second R) and General Thomas S. Power (R), commander in chief of the Strategic Air Command. 23rd March, 1962

"When power leads a man toward arrogance, poetry reminds him of his limitations. When power narrows the area of a man's concern, poetry reminds him of the richness and diversity of existence. When power corrupts, poetry cleanses."

Speech upon receiving an honorary degree, Amherst College, Amherst, Massachusetts, 26th October, 1963

Poet Robert Frost, celebrating his 88th birthday, is presented with the Congressional Medal by President John F. Kennedy at the White House in Washington, DC. 26th March, 1962

"Those who make peaceful revolution impossible will make violent revolution inevitable."

Address to Latin American diplomats at the White House, Washington, DC, 13th March, 1962

President John F. Kennedy makes a point during a news conference in Washington, DC.
29th March, 1962

"We stand for freedom. That is our conviction for ourselves; that is our only commitment to others."

President John F. Kennedy announces the appointment of Deputy Attorney General Byron White as Associate Justice of the Supreme Court.
30th March, 1962

"I think this is the most extraordinary collection of talent, of human knowledge, that has ever been gathered together at the White House, with the possible exception of when Thomas Jefferson dined alone."

Address at a reception honouring Nobel Prize winners at the White House, Washington, DC, April, 1962

President John F. Kennedy and President João Goulart of Brazil (second R) talk to news reporters outside the White House in Washington, DC. 4th April, 1962

"Law is the adhesive force in the cement of society, creating order out of chaos and coherence in place of anarchy."

Speech, Vanderbilt University, Nashville, Tennessee, 18th May, 1963

President John F. Kennedy meets representatives of the National Conference of State Legislative Leaders at the White House in Washington, DC.
11th April, 1962

"No one has been barred on account of his race from fighting or dying for America – there are no 'white' or 'colored' signs on the foxholes or graveyards of battle."

Message to Congress on proposed civil rights bill, 19th June, 1963

President John F. Kennedy checks out the view through the periscope of a nuclear submarine during an inspection of the vessel at the US naval base in Norfolk, Virginia. 13th April, 1962

"Geography has made us neighbours. History has made us friends. Economics has made us partners, and necessity has made us allies. Those whom God has so joined together, let no man put asunder."

Address to Canadian Parliament, 17th May, 1961

President John F. Kennedy and Canadian Ambassador Arnold D.P. Heeney enjoy a relaxed conversation in the president's office in the White House in Washington, DC.
17th April, 1962

"We have the power to make this the best generation of mankind in the history of the world or to make it the last."

Address to the UN General Assembly, New York, 20th September, 1963

President John F. Kennedy at his family home in Hyannis Port, Massachusetts, with his brothers Robert (second L) and Edward (second R), and attorney James Rowe. 23rd April, 1962

"Let us … step back from the shadows of war and seek out the way of peace. And if that journey is a thousand miles, or even more, let history record that we, in this land, at this time, took the first step."

Radio and TV address on the Limited Test Ban Treaty, July, 1963

President John F. Kennedy makes a point during a speech made at the dedication of the Nashville Avenue Wharf in New Orleans. 4th May, 1962

"Forgive your enemies, but never forget their names."

Quoted by Ed Koch in *Mayor*, 1984

President John F. Kennedy watches a practice alert for Strategic Air Command B52 bombers at Eglin Air Force Base, Florida. With him is USAF Chief of Staff General Curtis LeMay.
4th May, 1962

"If we cannot end now our differences, at least we can help make the world safe for diversity."

Speech, American University, Washington, DC, 10th June, 1963

President John F. Kennedy addresses the United Auto
Workers union in Atlantic City, New Jersey.
8th May, 1962

"I am certain that after the dust of centuries has passed over our cities, we, too, will be remembered not for victories or defeats in battle or in politics, but for our contribution to the human spirit."

Speaking on behalf of the National Cultural Center (later Kennedy Center), 29th November, 1962

President John F. Kennedy meets graduating cadets at the United States Military Academy at West Point in New York State. 6th June, 1962

"Tolerance implies no lack of commitment to one's own beliefs. Rather it condemns the oppression or persecution of others."

President John F. Kennedy with Cypriot leader Archbishop Makarios
following a conference at the White House in Washington, DC.
6th June, 1962

"The great enemy of the truth is very often not the lie – deliberate, contrived and dishonest – but the myth, persistent, persuasive and unrealistic. Belief in myths allows the comfort of opinion without the discomfort of thought."

Commencement Address, Yale University, New Haven, Connecticut, 11th June, 1962

President John F. Kennedy on his way to speak at Yale University's commencement ceremony, during which he was awarded an honorary law degree.
11th June, 1962

"The long labour of peace is an undertaking for every nation, and in this effort none of us can remain unaligned. To this goal none can be uncommitted."

Address to the UN General Assembly, New York, 20th September, 1963

President John F. Kennedy and Mexican President Adolfo Lopez Mateos
endure a blizzard of confetti as their motorcade drives along one of Mexico
City's boulevards at the start of Kennedy's official visit.
29th June, 1962

"I look forward to an America which will not be afraid of grace and beauty … an America which will reward achievement in the arts as we reward achievement in business or statecraft."

Speech upon receiving an honorary degree, Amherst College, Amherst, Massachusetts, 26th October, 1963

President John F. Kennedy and his wife Jacqueline stand to attention during the playing of the national anthem at a reception to herald the start of their official visit to Mexico. 30th June, 1962

"Liberty without learning is always in peril; learning without liberty is always in vain."

Speech, Vanderbilt University, Nashville, Tennessee, 18th May, 1963

President John F. Kennedy takes an important call from Washington on the speaker's platform during a campaign tour stop at McKeesport, Pennsylvania. 13th October, 1962

"Domestic policy can only defeat us; foreign policy can kill us."

President John F. Kennedy addresses the nation via TV and radio to announce that the United States will operate a naval blockade of Cuba until Soviet missiles are removed from the island.
22nd October, 1962

"I have a nice home, the office is close by and the pay is good."

Quoted by Kenneth O'Donnell, Dave Powers and Joseph McCarthy in
Johnny We Hardly Knew Ye, 1970

President John F. Kennedy and his wife Jacqueline during a
Christmas party for staff at the White House in Washington, DC.
12th December, 1962

"The men who create power make an indispensable contribution to the Nation's greatness, but the men who question power make a contribution just as indispensable, especially when that questioning is disinterested for they determine whether we use power or power uses us."

President John F. Kennedy addresses the House Chamber on Capitol Hill in Washington, DC. Vice President Lyndon B. Johnson is seated behind him.
14th January, 1963

"This country cannot afford to be materially rich and spiritually poor."

Message to Congress on the State of the Union, 14th January, 1963

Jo Grimond (L), leader of Britain's Liberal Party, in discussion with
President John F. Kennedy at the White House in Washington, DC.
14th January, 1963

"A nation reveals itself not only by the men it produces, but also by the men it honours, the men it remembers."

Speech upon receiving an honorary degree, Amherst College, Amherst, Massachusetts, 26th October, 1963

President John F. Kennedy presents the Young American medal for bravery to Philip Loura during a ceremony at the White House in Washington, DC. The 16-year-old had rescued two young girls from the icy water of a skating pond. 7th May, 1963

"The ignorance of one voter in a democracy impairs the security of all."

Speech, Vanderbilt University, Nashville, Tennessee, 18th May, 1963

President John F. Kennedy points out local landmarks to Canadian
Prime Minister Lester Pearson as the two sit on the terrace of the
president's summer home in Hyannis Port, Massachusetts.
10th May, 1963

"Only a respect for the law makes it possible for free men to dwell together in peace and progress."

Speech, Vanderbilt University, Nashville, Tennessee, 18th May, 1963

FBI Director J. Edgar Hoover meets with President John F. Kennedy in the president's office at the White House in Washington, DC. 10th May, 1963

SEAL OF THE PRESIDENT OF THE UNITED STATES

"Only an educated and informed people will be a free people."

Speech, Vanderbilt University, Nashville, Tennessee, 18th May, 1963

Reporters Frances Lewine (L) and Helen Thomas chat with
President John F. Kennedy after a White House press conference.
12th May, 1963

"My brother Bob doesn't want to be in government – he promised Dad he'd go straight."

Attorney General Robert Kennedy (L) with his brother President John F. Kennedy at the White House in Washington, DC. 15th May, 1963

"This nation has tossed its cap over the wall of space, and we have no choice but to follow it."

Remarks at the dedication of the Aerospace Medical Health Center,
San Antonio, Texas, 21st November, 1963

President John F. Kennedy with astronaut Gordon Cooper
(second R) during a White House reception.
21st May, 1963

"The best road to progress is freedom's road."

President John F. Kennedy and State Governor John Connally (L) along with other local officials take their places on a special platform erected at El Paso airport in Texas for a welcome ceremony for the president, who had flown in from the White Sands missile range in New Mexico.
5th June, 1963

"For in the final analysis, our most basic common link is that we all inhabit this small planet, we all breathe the same air, we all cherish our children's futures and we are all mortal."

Speech, American University, Washington, DC, 10th June, 1963

President John F. Kennedy and his son John, Jr, stand hand in hand at the White House in Washington, DC. 1963

"**What kind of peace do we seek? …
genuine peace, the kind of peace that
makes life on earth worth living, the kind
that enables men and nations to grow
and to hope and to build a better life for
their children – not merely peace for
Americans, but peace for all men and
women – not merely peace in our time,
but peace for all time.**"

Speech, American University, Washington, DC, 10th June, 1963

President John F. Kennedy delivers his Commencement
Address at American University in Washington, DC.
10th June, 1963

"I think 'Hail to the Chief' has a nice ring to it."

Reply when asked to name his favourite song, quoted by Noel Botham in
The Ultimate Book of Useless Information, 2007

President John F. Kennedy and West German Chancellor Konrad
Adenauer stand to attention while national anthems are played
following Kennedy's arrival at Bonn airport for an official visit.
23rd June, 1963

"Physical fitness is not only one of the most important keys to a healthy body, it is the basis of dynamic and creative intellectual activity."

President John F. Kennedy welcomes guests at a reception organised in his honour at the Palais Schaumburg in Bonn, West Germany. 23rd June, 1963

"Change is the law of life. And those who look only to the past or present are certain to miss the future."

Speech, Paulskirche, Frankfurt, West Germany, 25th June, 1963

President John F. Kennedy speaks at Roemerberg
Square, Frankfurt, West Germany.
25th June, 1963

"The United States, as the world knows, will never start a war. … This generation of Americans has already had enough – more than enough – of war and hate and oppression. We shall … do our part to build a world of peace where the weak are safe and the strong are just."

Speech, American University, Washington, DC, 10th June, 1963

President John F. Kennedy visits Checkpoint Charlie, the border crossing between West and East Berlin, a notable location during the Cold War. Behind him (hatless) is Mayor Willy Brandt.
26th June, 1963

"All free men, wherever they may live, are citizens of Berlin. And, therefore, as a free man, I take pride in the words *'Ich bin ein Berliner!'*"

Speech, Rathaus Schöneberg, West Berlin, Germany, 26th June, 1963

President John F. Kennedy addresses a large crowd
in front of Schöneberg city hall in West Berlin.
26th June, 1963

"The problems of the world cannot possibly be solved by sceptics or cynics whose horizons are limited by the obvious realities. We need men who can dream of things that never were and ask, 'Why not?'"

Address to the Irish Parliament, 28th June, 1963

A kiss of greeting from his cousin, Mrs Mary Ryan, brings a big smile to President John F. Kennedy's face during a visit to the home of his ancestors at Dunganstown, Ireland. 27th June, 1963

"I look forward to an America which commands respect throughout the world, not only for its strength, but for its civilisation as well. And I look forward to a world in which we will be safe not only for democracy and diversity, but also for personal distinction."

Speech upon receiving an honorary degree, Amherst College, Amherst, Massachusetts, 26th October, 1963

Caroline Kennedy, daughter of President John F. Kennedy, rests her head on her father's shoulder while aboard the presidential yacht *Honey Fitz* off the coast of Hyannis Port, Massachusetts. 31st August, 1963

"The effort to improve the conditions of man … is not a task for the few. It is the task of all nations … for plague and pestilence, and plunder and pollution, the hazards of nature and the hunger of children are the foes of every nation."

Address to the UN General Assembly, New York, 20th September, 1963

Walter Cronkite interviews President John F. Kennedy for a CBS News feature at the president's home in Hyannis Port, Massachusetts. 3rd September, 1963

"As we express our gratitude, we must never forget that the highest appreciation is not to utter words, but to live by them."

President John F. Kennedy applauds his younger brother, Senator Edward Kennedy of Massachusetts, during a Democratic Party fund-raising dinner in Boston, Massachusetts. 19th October, 1963

"Politics is like football; if you see daylight, go through the hole."

John Kennedy, Jr, discovers an interesting
feature of President John F. Kennedy's desk.
1963

"If anyone is crazy enough to want to kill a president of the United States, he can do it. All he must be prepared to do is give his life for the president's."

Above far left: A warm welcome in Dallas, Texas.
22nd November, 1963

Far left: The assassin, Lee Harvey Oswald.
22nd November, 1963

Above left: Riding the motorcade through Dallas, moments
before President Kennedy was shot.
22nd November, 1963

Left: Jacqueline and daughter Caroline say goodbye.
24th November, 1963

The Publishers gratefully acknowledge the Press Association and Associated Press, from whose extensive archives the photographs in this book have been selected.